Other titles in the series:
The World's Greatest Cat Cartoons
The World's Greatest Computer Cartoons
The World's Greatest Dad Cartoons

Published simultaneously in 1993 by Exley Publications
in Great Britain, and Exley Giftbooks in the USA.

Selection © Exley Publications Ltd.
The copyright for each cartoon remains with the cartoonist.

ISBN 1-85015-439-2

A copy of the CIP data is available from the British Library on request.
All rights reserved. No part of this publication may be reproduced
or transmitted in any form or by any means, electronic or mechanical,
including photocopy, recording or any information storage and
retrieval system without permission in writing from the publisher.

Front cover illustration by Roland Fiddy.
Designed by Pinpoint Design.
Edited by Mark Bryant.
Printed and bound by Grafo, S.A. – Bilbao, Spain.

Exley Publications Ltd, 16 Chalk Hill, Watford, Herts WD1 4BN,
United Kingdom.
Exley Giftbooks, 359 East Main Street, Suite 3D, Mount Kisco, NY
10549, USA.

Cartoons by Burgin, England, Gais, Graham, Langdon, Mahood,
Siggs, Starke, Thelwell, Wiles. HERMAN copyright Jim Unger.
Reprinted with permission of UNIVERSAL PRESS SYNDICATE.
All rights reserved.

THANK YOU

We would like to thank all the cartoonists who submitted entries for *The World's Greatest GOLF CARTOONS*. They came in from many parts of the world - including Holland, Canada the United Kingdom and the USA.

Special thanks go to the cartoonists whose work appears in the final book. They include Eric Burgin page 75; Clive Collins page 18; Douglas England page 13; Roland Fiddy cover, title page and pages 6, 8, 11, 19, 23, 26, 52, 55, 65; Noel Ford pages 28, 35, 38, 44, 54, 67; Gais page 31; Toni Goffe page 48; Alex Graham pages 4, 10, 50, 74, 76; Tony Husband pages 20, 21, 24, 33, 61, 68, 70, 79; David Langdon pages 42, 59, 71; Larry 25, 29, 30, 32, 49, 73; Kenneth Mahood page 41; David Myers pages 12, 34; Ken Pyne page 37; Hans Quist pages 14, 22, 43, 51, 53; Bryan Reading pages 45, 72; Siggs page 36; Mike Scott pages 5, 7, 9, 62, 66, 78; Leslie Starke pages 17, 40, 47, 63; Bill Stott pages 16, 27, 46, 60, 69; Norman Thelwell pages 39, 64, 77; Dean Vietor pages 56, 57, 58; Arnold Wiles page 15.

Every effort has been made to trace the copyright holders of cartoons in this book. However any error will gladly be corrected by the publisher for future printings.

THE WORLD'S GREATEST

GOLF

CARTOONS

EDITED BY
Mark Bryant

EXLEY
MT. KISCO, NEW YORK · WATFORD, UK

"Put it off? Because of a little shower?"

5

"Look at those idiots — fishing in this weather!"

DAMMIT! I FORGOT TO WISH MURIEL A MERRY CHRISTMAS THIS MORNING!

"I suppose this means we'll have to cut across to the fifth."

"Sometimes I feel nobody cares a jot about me."

"What did I say after . . . our closest attention to the matter in hand'?"

"Relax. This isn't going to take long ..."

"You really need something to take your mind off your hobby."

"He uses golf to unwind . . ."

"*I sneezed when my Daddy was taking a putt...*"

— CLIVE COLLINS —

"Scuse me, may we play through?"

"Don't think Gerry was too pleased with me questioning his score at the end, do you?"

"Will you never learn not to ask your father how his golf went, when he comes home early?"

"He was caught wearing spikes in the clubhouse."

"I don't care how original it is — unfair play is unfair play!"

"Sorry to hear the bad news June —
listen, will you be selling your clubs?"

"Frankly, business could be better."

"Better look busy — the old man's about."

"I know that expression — he's hooked a nice fat order."

"His handicap is that he doesn't realize that he should let his boss win."

"Believe it or not, Peterson, at first I was totally opposed to an open-plan office system."

"How do you like being on the board of directors, Wilkins?"

"Amalgamated's goods may be shoddy, and their delivery dates
unreliable, but their chief executive knows when to concede a putt!"

41

*"You don't imagine I actually **enjoy** this aspect of my work?"*

"No, the General Manager went out about twenty minutes ago,
but I'm expecting him back any minute!"

"I wish to thank you for my gift. I will think of you all, every time I use them to unblock the drains!"

45

"Dear God. Thank you for encouraging my wife to take up golf.
Please don't ever let her get better than me . . ."

"I was standing too close to the ball, my grip was all wrong,
I wasn't keeping my head down, and what else...?"

48

50

"Well, she wasn't too keen on it, but at long last she said I could go."

"Have I or haven't I stayed at home to help you
in the garden — yes or no?"

"Goodnight, Helen — I take it I'll be hearing no more of this 'I'm leaving you' nonsense."

YOUR GOLF GAME'S IN BIG TROUBLE WHEN...
... your slice starts to look good to you.

YOUR GOLF GAME'S IN BIG TROUBLE WHEN...
... you never lose any balls because you never hit them very far.

YOUR GOLF GAME'S IN BIG TROUBLE WHEN...
... *you're getting bigger laughs than Johnny Carson.*

"Beautiful, Sir. One of these days we'll let you try it with a ball."

"I'm good at golf. I can feel it inside of me.
It just never comes out whilst I'm playing."

"Skied that one didn't you."

"Hurry up. Other people are waiting to use the bunker."

"Er... thank you!"

"Mr. Finnington — almost anyone can learn to play golf.
Unfortunately — you're an almost."

"And to think that fifty thousand dollars depend on a grown man
getting that stupid little ball into that fatuous little hole in the ground."

"I used to play at a Scottish club, but it had to close down when they lost the ball."

"What do you think? A three iron or a four wood?"

"Do you really? What's your handicap?"

"Now this is Heaven!"

Books in "The World's Greatest" series
($4.99 £2.99 paperback)

The World's Greatest Cat Cartoons
The World's Greatest Computer Cartoons
The World's Greatest Dad Cartoons
The World's Greatest Golf Cartoons

Books in the "Victim's Guide" series
($4.99 £2.99 paperback)

Award winning cartoonist Roland Fiddy sees the funny side to life's phobias, nightmares and catastrophes.

The Victim's Guide to the Dentist
The Victim's Guide to the Doctor
The Victim's Guide to Middle Age

Books in the "Crazy World" series
($4.99 £2.99 paperback)

The Crazy World of Aerobics (Bill Stott)
The Crazy World of Cats (Bill Stott)
The Crazy World of Cricket (Bill Stott)
The Crazy World of Gardening (Bill Stott)
The Crazy World of Golf (Mike Scott)
The Crazy World of the Greens (Barry Knowles)
The Crazy World of The Handyman (Roland Fiddy)
The Crazy World of Hospitals (Bill Stott)
The Crazy World of Housework (Bill Stott)
The Crazy World of the Leaner Driver (Bill Stott)
The Crazy World of Love (Roland Fiddy)

The Crazy World of Marriage (Bill Stott)
The Crazy World of Rugby (Bill Stott)
The Crazy World of Sailing (Peter Rigby)
The Crazy World of Sex (David Pye)

Books in the "Fanatics" series
($4.99 £2.99 paperback)

The **Fanatic's Guides** are perfect presents for everyone with a hobby that has got out of hand. Eighty pages of hilarious black and white cartoons by Roland Fiddy

The Fanatic's Guide to the Bed
The Fanatic's Guide to Cats
The Fanatic's Guide to Computers
The Fanatic's Guide to Dads
The Fanatic's Guide to Diets
The Fanatic's Guide to Dogs
The Fanatic's Guide to Husbands
The Fanatic's Guide to Money
The Fanatic's Guide to Sex
The Fanatic's Guide to Skiing

Great Britain: Order these super books from your local bookseller or from Exley Publications Ltd, 16 Chalk Hill, Watford, Herts WD1 4BN. (Please send £1.30 to cover post and packaging on 1 book, £2.60 on 2 or more books.)